THE
GOOD
IN MY
AFFLICTIONS

By: Dorreth Mitchell

Dorreth Mitchell

The GOOD in My Afflictions

© 2016 by Dorreth Mitchell

Published in United States of America

Scripture quotations marked "KJV" are taken from the Holy Bible, King James Version, Cambridge, 1769. Bible quotations are extensively used in this book. They are highlighted to show distinction from the remaining text.

Dedication and Acknowledgements

Without the love of the Father, the grace of His Son, and the guidance of the Spirit none of this would be possible. To my son Pastor Mirthell Mitchell and my daughter-in-law Rita, thank you for your diligent support and encouragement, in editing, formatting and giving me ideas in writing this book.

I also dedicate this book to my late son Pedro, my daughter Rosia, son-in-law Anthony, and to all my grandchildren Anthony, Maria, Shalom, Sinead, Sade, and Shiloh. I encourage you to continue to love Jesus and give Him first place in your lives.

To Clover, Joe, Lewanna, Gloria, Arthur, Cheryl, and all my closest family and friends, too many to name them all; to my church family at Brampton SDA and North West Brampton SDA, the Ontario Conference Sisterhood of pastor's wives, I thank-you for all the love and support.

To my mother Amelia Finnegan and my husband Pastor Carlton Mitchell, who both fell asleep in Christ, I dedicate this book in memory of your sacrifices, love, and example shown to us.

Table of Contents

Introduction

"It is good for me that I was afflicted."
Psalm 119:71

This book is not so much about the trials and tribulations I have experienced in my life, but rather it is a story of my triumph. How I found hope when there was no earthly reason to hope. How I navigated through grief, without utterly being destroyed. I am sharing intimate details of my story with you, because everyone will experience loss, heartache, trials, pain, or suffering of some degree in their life time; but how many people will say like David *"it is good for me that I was afflicted."* Psalm 119:71

I have heard this saying used over and over again that life is an endless pain with a painful end. I beg to differ, I have enjoyed much of my life but it was not void of painful circumstances. Nevertheless, I totally can relate that life's journey has difficult experiences beyond our control. Sometimes even our best made plans go wrong.

God's plan is for our lives to be used to bring honor and glory to His name and a blessing to those we come in contact with on our journey. Our journey may consist of rivers to cross, mountains to climb, and crude winter weather as we run this race towards our eternal destination. The purpose of life is to prepare us for eternity. These challenges we experience as we journey, are there to build our character fitting us to live with a Holy and righteous God.

Like most journeys, depending on if we have the right tools, it becomes easier for us to get where we are going. The necessary tools all depends on the terrain. If it is a road trip then a map or better yet a GPS would be the most effective tool. If the journey takes you off road through mountains or the wilderness then a compass and a survival kit will be needed. The same is true for life itself, I have come to realize that suffering is an essential part of this journey. I have learned how to triumph over trials, and I would like to share with you the ways in which you can also.

Imagine walking alone through a valley, or perhaps a poorly lit alley. You get the ominous sense that you are being followed. You can feel death, and darkness surrounding you. You dare not turn to face it, but you see its giant shadow climbing the wall beside you. Shadows are darker and can be much larger than the object itself. Just imagine whatever death looks like, its shadow must be that much more terrifying. So when David penned this popular metaphor thousands of years ago *"Yea though I walk through the valley of the shadow of death..."* Psalms 23. He was attempting to portray life's darkest moments for him, using one of the scariest imagery he could imagine, the shadow of death.

But there is so much more that David shares with us in the text. When we look deeper into the life of David and into this brief biblical narrative what we find are the remarkable ways in which David becomes triumphant over tribulations despite the circumstances. David moves us beyond the unimaginable pain, suffering, and loss.

In the text, there is something greater than the darkness, greater and infinitely stronger than shadows. There is something bigger and ultimately supreme over the valley itself. David's great revelation is that *"I will fear no evil, for thou art with me…"* Psalms 23. David takes us beyond the shadows into God's marvelous light.

David intentionally uses shadows because of its very nature. Shadows are dark areas that take shape when a body comes between rays of light and a surface. Evil attempts to come between God and us, but God only permits it to cast shadows. Shadows that cannot last. As scary as shadows can be, shadows themselves are harmless. As soon as David realizes that the light of the world is with him, he no longer fears the evil that is trying to get in between.

So there it is, the entire point of this book; God is with you, and with Him there is nothing you cannot overcome! With God's presence, comes God's protection, His provision, and His providence. So what is the point to write anything further?

Truthfully God is with each of us, but for lack of knowledge many prolong their suffering. For lack of knowledge some even perish, where there was a clear path towards deliverance. Like David, it is my desire to lead you beyond my darkest moments, pass the trials and tribulation, and show you HOW to strengthen your relationship with God during these most difficult times.

Remember we need the right tools for whatever journey we are embarking upon, whether through the valley of relational shadows, personal development shadows, and even the shadows of death.

The question is, how can we find blessings in our loss, in our suffering, in our pain, in our troubles, in our disappointments, in our despair? How can we get to that point in believing and accepting that, *"All things work together for good to them that love God and are called according to His purposes?"* *Romans 8:28*. As you read this book you will come to realize that we serve an awesome God that never makes a mistake.

This is why in the next few chapters I not only share the actual stories of my pain and loss, but I also describe my emotional journey. I reveal private diary entries that document my interactions with God, and his amazing answers to my prayers. I wanted you, the reader, to get an accurate account of the live experience.

If you are facing a difficult time now with the loss of a love one in death or dealing with the challenges of life, let me share with you what God has done for me. My painful experiences and adversities have served to draw me into a growing and fulfilling relationship with my Lord and Savior Jesus Christ, and for this I can be thankful.

Chapter 1
My First Love

"You have persevered and have endured hardships for my name, and have not grown weary.4 Yet I hold this against you: You have forsaken your first love."
Revelation 2:3, 4

Looking back I can say it was special to have known my husband since primary school. Carlton and I attended Eccleston Primary School in Aboukir district, St Ann Jamaica, West Indies. Back then, his nickname was Bob and my nickname was P, for Ponds Crème. We actually sat in the same class since kindergarten, but to tell you the truth I hardly noticed him back then. Little did I know I had a secret admirer, who would spend much of the class period watching me from his desk. Year after year with each grade we advanced, he relayed to me how he would daydream about approaching me and asking me to be his girlfriend. He would say to himself "Maybe today I will talk to P." "Maybe if I sit directly behind her I can play with her long flowing hair." It wasn't much of a secret, everyone else seemed to know about his affections except for me. But the years grew faster than his courage.

At 12 years old, Carlton left the district for high school after having been awarded a scholarship to attend Holmwood Technical School in Manchester Jamaica. I also left for high school in the city of Kingston, Jamaica. The very first time I took notice of him was the Sunday he caught up with me after church was dismissed. I had attended the Methodist church which was only a block from my house. We were both home for holidays from high school. Although he and his parents were members of the Anglican Church, he confessed later he visited my church just to see me.

Bob was a smooth young man with slick words. He relayed this experience from his perspective, "As I sat in church the songs were a blur, the prayers were a blur, the sermon was a blur, yet still it was as though I were in heaven; one thing was clear, I was sitting in the aisle across from an angel in all her beauty." He must have thought I was very religious because that day it was as though I was eating up every word that the minister was saying. Little did he know, as he was admiring me, I was admiring the pastor. I always daydreamed about marrying a minister and I would be a nurse. We would have a family and live happily ever after. The problem was that the only pastor I knew was this older Methodist minister who was already married.

Since Bob could not get my attention during church he made sure that he would talk to me after church. After church as I was walking home, Bob ran and caught up with me. Being a small community I knew his family, and I knew who he was, but I really never noticed him beyond that. Besides Bob was no pastor. So it took me by surprise when Bob said "this might not mean much to you right now but I love you and I want to marry you when I grow up." I thought to myself "What is this boy talking about!" But something significant happened that day; Bob went from virtually being invisible in my eyes to being ridiculously visible. But to Bob at least he was finally noticed. We were both 15 at the time; it wasn't until a few years later that I saw him again. This time Bob came over to my house.

I was in my room that was adjacent to the living room. I knew my parents had company over but I paid little attention to the conversation as people from the neighborhood often stopped by unannounced to chat. The guest was there for hours chatting with my parents until my father called for me. "P, please bring the lamp and escort young Mr. Mitchell outside so he can see his way down the porch stairs." Then I realized it was Bob again. I thought "That ridiculous young man whom I barely have said two words to, but thinks he's going to marry me. LOL."

Bob didn't have much time to speak; he had to get the words out quickly, for back in those days it was not proper for a young man to be talking to a young woman alone outside the company of others, especially on a dark night. So he quickly asked me where I was staying in Kingston so that he might visit me there on his next visit. I told him 26 Gardenia Ave, Mona Heights, Kingston, Jamaica. Bob did not have a pen and paper so he sang 26 Gardeeenia Ave, 2-6 Gardeeeenia Avenuuuue, 26 Gardeeeenia Avenuuuue, all the way home.

Little did I know Bob had written a letter asking my parents' permission for our friendship. By then we were both working in the city of Kingston. We dated for three years before we got married. My original plan was to go to England to study nursing, but that plan became secondary and was placed on hold. Another plan I put out of my mind was to marry a minister, for I now had a new dream man. I had fallen in love with Bob. Now all grown up Carlton was now officially my boyfriend.

While living in Kingston we both started to attend the Roman Catholic Church, and would go every Sunday to mass. Carlton needed to find a place to live closer to work. He so happened to meet a longtime friend, who needed someone to share a flat. This friend's grandparents happened to also be the landlord and they were Seventh-day Adventist Christians. As time progressed the Morgans would invite Carlton to their worship service on Friday evenings. When I would visit with him I would also sit in the worship service to welcome the Sabbath.

One day the Morgans invited him to church and he attended. He thought he went just to be polite. The Holy Spirit took control of both his mind as well as mine as the Morgans gave us bible studies and prepared us for baptism. This was a direct providence of the leading of God in our lives. Soon we were both baptized and became members of the Rollington Town Seventh-day Adventist Church.

Three months after our baptism, Carlton and I solidified our commitment to each other in marriage. We got married on the 28th of February 1971 in the Rollington Seventh-day Adventist church, Jamaica, West Indies.

It was a bright sunny Sunday morning when I looked into the eyes of my best friend and made that promise to have and to hold for better or for worse, for richer or poorer, in sickness and in health, to love and to cherish till death do us part. I meant every bit of these words; little did I know I would be challenged on every element of our vows sooner than I would have imagined.

But let the cares of tomorrow worry about itself, for this day my heart sang with joy as I celebrated with friends, my family and church family. The celebration took place at the home of Grandma and Grandpa Morgan. Tables and chairs were set up in the yard and it was a grand celebration. We had just given our hearts to God in the watery grave of baptism, and now we had given our hearts to each other. We embarked upon our new found faith in Christ with the passion, zeal and sincere determination to serve our God and be faithful to each other till death.

We enjoyed our new found faith as Seventh-day Adventist Christians and looked forward to meeting at the home of Grandpa and Grandma Morgan who were instrumental in leading us to know Jesus in a more sincere way. It was beautiful to be able to grow to know each other better and also to have that connection with our God.

We were married for about six months, but life in Jamaica, with the desire to get ahead, was challenging. My husband had expressed an interest to travel to the United States to pursue a career in graphic arts. He had already applied for a visa prior to us getting married, but was unsuccessful. I did not anticipate this happening any time soon, neither did I care. After all we were now married and expecting a baby on the way. This was certainly not a good time to think about travelling to the USA.

Things were getting tougher every day. We could only afford to rent one bed room in a shared flat. We had to share the kitchen and the rest of the living area with three other couples. With me expecting a baby on the way it was not an ideal setting.

I tried getting a job, but I only lasted one week because of morning sickness. I observed and could see my husband was in deep thoughts. Soon we had to make plans in getting a bigger place to accommodate our baby on the way.

His salary was not enough to accommodate a bigger place so we came to the decision for me to go back to my parents place and stay with them until the baby was born. He would then visit every weekend and fortunately we are from the same town so his parents were also close by.

I felt comfortable with this decision so the move was made. Back in my parents' home I got the support and training I so well needed from both parents as an inexperienced mother-to-be. Just as I was starting to get comfortable with seeing my husband every weekend and getting excited to welcome our bundle of joy in our life - my heart was crushed and my bubble burst. My husband visited that last weekend and broke the news. "Honey I got the visa and I am leaving for the U.S. on Monday!" "What do you mean tomorrow; this Monday?

I could not believe his excitement. Here I was having his baby less than one year married and he is excited to run off and leave me! "I am hurt, I can't believe you can be so excited about leaving me at a time like this!"

He explained, "Honey, it's not about leaving you, it's an opportunity for us as a family. As soon as the baby is born and I am settled, you both will be able to join me, and you can also get a student visa. (EASIER SAID THAN DONE)

Why God, why now? How can this possibly be good for my family? I felt a feeling of loss, like I would never see my husband again.

We hugged and I cried, the tears kept flowing. He promised to write me every week. He reassured me he loved me and that this was for our best, he wanted to make a better life for our family.

My husband left for the USA within a month after I returned to live with my parents. There was no telephone available back then in that part of the country where I lived, so I looked forward to getting a letter every week from him. He was faithful to his word. I could not understand how he found the time to do so with working part-time and going to school full-time. This was the highlight of my week, getting a letter from my husband. Nevertheless I still could not imagine that this temporary separation could be so painful. I got words of encouragement from some and discouragement from others, such as, "you may never see him again!" or "he is too young to be by himself!" "By the time you get to join him, he would have another woman and child in his life." I had heard so many stories of this happening to others, would he forget me?

Even if he forgot me I could never forget him. He was my first love, he would be my only love.

"You have persevered and have endured hardships for my name, and have not grown weary.
4 Yet I hold this against you: You have forsaken your first love."
Revelation 2:3, 4

Jesus reminds us that those new in the faith will experience hardships, and that the hardship should not cause us to forsake our first love. Too often those in the faith, especially new believers fail to see the hidden blessings in hardship. Why? Because we misinterpret hardship as God abandoning us, thinking that we have lost favor with Him. We begin to focus on perseverance in that particular matter and not growing weary, in order to win back God's favor. In doing so we may have many spiritual gains, but unfortunately lose our first love, a close personal relationship with God Himself. Why is this the case? Well let's ask this question.

What is the formula for a successful relationship with God? Is it how good we are or is it how perfect His love is towards us? The correct answer is actually none of the above. The formula for a successful relationship with God is us remembering and being moved by God's perfect love towards us. God's love is marginalized in our life if we distort His character. This is why I say, whether we have caused the suffering on ourselves or not, one thing is certain, God permits suffering in our life as an opportunity to draw us closer to Him, not push us further away. God in his wisdom senses our greater need of our dependency on Him, and permits hardship as one of the means of drawing us closer to Him.

When we accurately accept and respond to the true nature of God's love for us, it is one of the ways that we draw closer to God and it pleases Him. The bible calls that faith.

"Without faith it is impossible to please Him, because anyone that comes to God must believe that He is and that He rewards those who earnestly seek Him."

Hebrews 11:6

Faith is not just knowing that He is, the advancing of our faith is believing that He loves you and wants the best for you. I have come to know that faith does not mean everything will go the way we plan, it means when we place faith in God we are submitting to God's plan. The hardest part of submitting to God's plan, especially in the beginning, is that it does not look familiar at all to what we desire for our own lives. I was hurting because I did not want to be alone at my mother's house, with a child, and without my husband. I felt like I was going backward not forward. Whatever happened to my dream of being a nurse and marrying a pastor?

If only I had known that this incoming crisis was actually for my good. I could have been stronger through it. I would have been less concerned about the negative things that could transpire because of the separation in my marriage, and focus rather on the positive things that would be developed in my union with God. The blessing I now see in the adversity of separation from my husband was that his absence served to draw me closer to God and increased my commitment to love Him despite the odds.

What are you going through today that is an opportunity to strengthen your love and appreciation for God? How is God calling you closer to him? How can faith strengthen your relationship with God today? I have not forgotten my first love, much in part due to my past sufferings.

Chapter 2
What Can Separate Us?

*"For I am convinced that neither death nor life,
neither angels nor demons, neither the present nor
the future, nor any powers, 39 neither height nor
depth, nor anything else in all creation, will be
able to separate us from the love of God that is in
Christ Jesus our Lord."*
Romans 8:38

After my baby boy was born, I sent Carlton photos
and he was so elated. Pedro, our son, looked just
like him. After my baby was six months old, we
tried the possibility of applying for a student visa.
While waiting I decided to apply for a job in the city
of Kingston. I eventually had to leave my young son
with my parents to be cared for by them.

Money was tight and my husband was working only
enough to keep up paying his tuition and living
expenses in the United States. Thanks be to God, I
immediately got a temporary job, in the city of
Kingston. Not long after, I got a more suitable job
at Andrews Memorial Hospital in the accounts
department. I was very happy I was able to work
and support my son and not be totally dependent on
my parents. I missed my son but stood to my
responsibility of work so he could have the
necessities of life. My parents and parents-in-law
were very supportive.

When my son was six months old I brought him to Kingston and had him dedicated in the very church we both got married in. My son was now eleven months old. Our application for my visa for the USA was turned down. While absence makes the heart grow fonder, sustained absence from my husband was now causing my heart unimaginable pain. Now Carlton was also feeling emotional pain as he was becoming more discouraged with the circumstances. He soon asked his sister Clover who had migrated to Canada to send me a letter of invitation, which she promptly did.

Things did not work in my favor to go to the United States, but God works in mysterious ways, wonders to perform. My sister-in-law Clover who had migrated to Canada almost a year already, extended an invitation for me to come to Canada for a visit.

It was already almost a year since my husband had left, for the U.S. so I gladly took her up on the offer. I arrived in Canada in July 1972. My son Pedro became one years old a few days after I arrived in Canada. I was very sad having missed his first birthday. But being in Canada, renewed my hope in my family being reunited someday. What a grand reunion it was when my husband and I reconnected for the first time at Niagara Falls after crossing over from the United States.

After meeting my husband at Niagara Falls he was able to cross the border into Canada with his student visa. We spent one week together before his return back to the United States. This was truly like a second honeymoon. I was on cloud nine and thankful to God for bringing us together again. There was no way I would now return to Jamaica, with him being able to drive to Canada to see me. With this easy access of us seeing each other, I applied for my stay in Canada. I was immediately placed on a waiting list.

After a few months of waiting to hear from the Canadian immigration I was granted a temporary work permit. Thank God I was able to work to support my son. I was also grateful that my parents kept me connected to my son through regular photo shots of him. Each time I got a new photo I would shed a tear and wish I could hold him in my arms.

All these blessings were not without some challenges. While I was closer to my husband, I was further from my son. I felt broken into pieces, a part of me in Canada, a part of me in the United States and a part of me in Jamaica.

A few months after my husband return to the United States I started to experience morning sickness and I missed my monthly cycle. On a visit to the doctor, I learned I was pregnant. This time with my daughter. Needless to say the timing was not right for us, but sometimes God works His greatest miracles with our untimely circumstances.

When it was time for my daughter to be born, my husband visited for a week. My husband was now able to take part in the birth of our second child and this was a delight for both of us. Rosia was born on April 7, 1973. Carlton stayed a week with me and then had to return to the United States.

It was a delight when I left the hospital with my bundle of joy. It was very hard though not having the support of my husband by my side. I felt alone and cheated out of the joy of my dream of a family. However I stood strong and remained prayerful. I was allowed eight weeks from my job for maternity leave. I did my best to care for my daughter, she brought me much joy. The challenge I now faced was, what would I do with my baby once I return to work? I dreaded having to take her out to a babysitter in the cold and without access to a vehicle of my own.

As I was praying and planning, my mother-in-law came to Canada for a visit. Talk about an answer to prayer and God's perfect timing. Jeremiah 1:5 says *"before I formed thee in the belly I knew thee, and before thou camest forth out of the womb, I sanctified thee..."* God had this plan formulated and set in place before I even got pregnant. We serve a mighty and caring God who cares about the minutest affair of the children of this earth. Nothing is hidden from His eyes. My mother-in-law stayed a few weeks and upon leaving she took my daughter with her to Jamaica.

It broke my heart to see my baby leave, but I was consoled to know she was in the caring hands of her grandmother. However, I missed that mother-daughter bond which is so essential in the early years of a child's life.

I consoled myself that both children were together and would have an opportunity to bond as siblings and despite me or my husband not being there we did the best we could, given the situation. I returned to work being thankful that I could at least provide the essentials of life for them and with a plan in mind that my family would be together soon.

Yes life does have rivers to cross, mountains to climb, rocks that will stub our toes, but in all of these, take heart because God desires to bless us and what may seem like setbacks are actually teaching us to trust God's providence, His sovereignty and plans. *"Trust in The Lord with all thine heart and lean not unto thine own understanding; in all thy ways acknowledge Him, and He shall direct thy paths."* Proverbs 3:5, 6. We need to let our hearts perceive what our eyes are unable to see.

Carlton had a heart for helping others. When he was in Jamaica, one of his kind deeds towards a tourist from New York was now repaying him tenfold. He was able to stay at their home while working and preparing to go into school. The plan was for him to get into the printing press business and make enough money to sponsor his family to join him.

It so happened that one day while Carlton was doing his part time evening job at McDonalds. He and one other worker were responsible for closing. They were held up by two bandits who forced their way in when his coworker went out to empty the trash. One of the bandits held a gun at Carlton's head while the other had a knife at his coworker's neck. His coworker was being forced to open up the cash register but somehow had difficulty doing so. Because he wasn't fast enough, the man that had the gun at Carlton's head became agitated and distracted, so he went over and threatened to shoot the guy for stalling. At this juncture, Carlton dashed from the scene, and ran around the corner, kicking the side door open as though he went out, but instead dashed down to the basement and hid in the freezer. This distracted the thieves as they quickly grabbed the cash, they too ran outside, but were unaware of where Carlton had ran so fast. Thinking that Carlton, who was now gone, could be alerting the authorities, they left both Carlton and his coworker unharmed. When the authorities arrived to investigate one of the police officers asked Carlton where he was from. He told him Jamaica. He said "I figured, in New York, you never run from a gunman. You have someone watching over you."

Carlton knew that God was watching over him, because not too long before, he had a vision of Jesus in his room. Jesus was calling him, but for what exactly? At that time it was not clear. It felt so real that he was uncertain whether he was in fact sleeping or awake. But after this incident, God would make His calling on Carlton's life clear.

That night when the news of the robbery got to the couple where he lodged, they encouraged him to leave that job. The gentleman who was like a father figure to him told him you are such a God fearing man; a man with such high principles, you should prepare yourself for ministry, have you ever considered this? This gave Carlton food for thought and so he immediately sent his transcripts to Atlantic Union College in Massachusetts along with a resume from the pastor of his church in New York. He started his undergrad studies towards pastoral ministry the following semester.

At the time I hadn't even realized that God was all along working on my dream of marrying a minister. All I had known was that I had married my childhood sweetheart, but God knew all along that I was marrying His servant, who would soon be hired into full-time pastoral ministry. God's plan was now taking shape. My husband and I were geographically much closer now. He could drive up to the New York, Niagara Falls border, and visit me from time to time. He was now in school to become a pastor.

With the help of his sister Clover, who assisted me in getting an immigration lawyer, I applied for landed status. In doing so I was also informed that I would be able to apply for my husband after having obtained a permanent stay. Canada, not the United States, would be the place where our family would live. There were a few Adventist congregations in Toronto, so there was a possibility that Carlton could be hired after he graduated.

I was hopeful. But the process seemed to be taking forever. You see I had now gotten accustomed to a regular visit from Carlton. He had already visited on three occasions. His last visit was just before his mother returned to Jamaica with our daughter. He was on his way here for his fourth visit, when he called me from the border to tell me that he was detained by immigration and was not allowed to cross the border. Something needed to be clarified with his student visa. When he told me I became scared and felt helpless. My only resolve was to pray and leave it to God. I thank God that they only prevented him from coming across rather than deporting him. I became desperate in my desire to have my husband even just to visit. I sought help from Pastor Manley Coleman who at that time was an elder at West Toronto church where I attended. He was a very spiritual and caring father in Zion. When I related my situation, and told him how desperate I was to have my family with me. I told him that maybe it was best for us both to return to Jamaica. I knew Carlton did not want to go back to Jamaica, he wanted to continue on his path towards the ministry in the United States. But I could not take being apart from my husband and children any longer.

I was not simply being emotional or impulsive; along with my desire to have my family together I was also vulnerable as a female in my early twenties, living all alone in a strange new country. Back then I did not wear a wedding band, so when the opposite sex would approach me, it was repulsive and frustrating when men would persist. I had to make it explicitly clear that I was happily married and not interested.

However on three different occasions when my apartment got broken into during the daytime it was quite scary. You see I would work the night shift and sleep during the day, but these particular times I was out at appointments. I had nothing in my home to steal, it was empty. For thieves to break in once I could understand, but the policeman doing the investigation said "three times means they are looking for something other than to steal."

All these things drove me to my knees. Some nights in my small apartment, with a broken radiator, I would get so cold. One night, cold and scared, I got down on my knees crying to God in prayer once again, only to wake up many hours later at 2:00am still on my knees. I was praying for the warmth of my husband beside me. Not just for warmth but also for protection.

I remember walking home one evening carrying several bags of groceries during a blizzard. It was so cold I thought I would turn into a pillar of ice. One of my bags broke, and in utter frustration and desperation I just dropped all my bags right there in the street, and walked away. Truth be told I was broken, and I just wanted to walk away from my current situation and just go home to warm Jamaica, with my family all together. Maybe I could take matters into my own hands to get him deported, and then I could meet him back in Jamaica with our children. At least we would be all together again as a family. By this time, my husband had started the theology degree at Atlantic Union College in Boston, completing his first year to become a pastor. Brother Coleman as he was then called, discouraged that idea, warning me "never stand in the way of your husband's calling". He arranged to take me to the immigration office the next day.

The immigration officer checked my files and told me that my name was way down on the list, and it would take more than a year to get to my name. I left the office in tears, frustrated and disappointed. I never forgot what Brother Coleman said to me that day, "Do you believe God can remove mountains? He is a God of the impossible, just trust Him". Those words of assurance resonate with me to this date. He then prayed with me and asked God to hasten the process. If granted, this would mean that I could then apply for Carlton's status in Canada.

As a test to my faith, Carlton received a notice from the American government that said he would be deported on a given date. We knew that he could not cross the border into Canada as he had recently been turned back. If he tried now, they would deport him even earlier than the date given and we certainly did not want a stamp of deportation to be reflected on his passport. It's funny how first I had prayed for him to be deported, now I was praying that he would not!

Every day Carlton went to the mailroom waiting for any notice from the Canadian government for his invitation, but nothing came. The date came for Carlton to be deported back to Jamaica from the United States. On his way to the airport he went to the mailroom to check one more time. It was Friday the 13th. The mailman who had now gotten to know him, said to Carlton "come back Monday, today would be bad luck to check for the notice." Carlton said "I believe in God not superstition, please check this last time." Sure enough, God came through right in time. Instead of driving to the airport Carlton drove across the border into Canada, into our home, and into my arms. The God of the impossible answered my prayers. This is the same God. Creator of Heaven and Earth that I continue to serve and trust today. Philippians 4:6 admonishes us *"Do not be anxious about anything, but in everything, by prayer and petition, with thanksgiving, present your request to God."*

While Carlton was on a student visa in the U. S., he had worked part time at Sears in the parts department. Upon his arrival here in Canada, he immediately applied for a position at Sears. He was able to get a job in the parts department at Sears in Rexdale. Having my husband by my side was truly a dream fulfilled. We could now consider bringing our children back from Jamaica to join us.

Only a few months after he started this job, while at work one day, he received the sad news that his mother, who was never ill, had died suddenly. This was a sudden shock to the both of us. We were not prepared for this either emotionally or financially. We had just used all our little savings to buy an old second hand car in preparation for our children's arrival. Thank God that in the midst of our troubles, God always has a solution. He is always one step ahead of us in our trials.

We told our church family about our predicament. One Good Samaritan gave Carlton some money. He then paid his fare and attended his mother's funeral. My mother-in-law died on January 19, 1975. Soon after Carlton returned from attending his mother's funeral, he received some more bad news. His eldest brother Aston then 27 years old, died on February 4, 1975.

We were not yet through the grief of his mother and to make matters worse, because of financial restraint he could not attend the funeral. It was painful for both of us that we could not even attend.

Only God could have taken us through the pain of these losses. Little did we know that sudden, multiple deaths, and of lives taken away too young would revisit our family soon.

At the time I could only think about the book of Job when he was going through all his troubles and he proclaimed, *"man that is born of a woman is of few days, and full of troubles"* Job 14:1. Just when things seems to be going well, we are reminded don't get too comfortable now. But God wants for us to still trust Him in the good times as well as in the bad times. So when the trials of life knock us down, whether through the death of a loved one, divorce, financial setbacks or whatever you are faced with, cry out to God, He hears our cry. Psalm 55:22 says *"cast your burdens upon The Lord and He will sustain you; He will never allow the righteous to be shaken".* Let us keep in persistent prayer and fight the good fight of faith. God will certainly see us through, He is our Burden Bearer.

By the summer of 1975, my children had arrived from Jamaica. They were accompanied by my brother Joseph on his visit to Canada. My son was 4 years old and my daughter 2 years old. It was a joy to have my family united as one. Luke 18:7-8 says *"and shall not God avenge His own elect, which cry day and night unto him, though he bear long with them? I tell you that he will avenge them speedily."* Despite what we go through God has promised to transform our dark yesterdays. He has promised us in Romans 8:28 that *"all things work together for good to those who love God and have been called according to his purpose."*

One of the best ways to persevere during trying times, when you are tempted to believe that God has turned his back on you, is to claim His promises and trust God because, God cannot lie. During these trying times I became familiar with God's promises and I learned to claim them daily. When you replace God's word with your circumstance, God's word becomes your reality.

One of my favorite promises is Romans 8

> *"I consider that our present sufferings are not worth comparing with the glory that will be revealed in us...* *25 But if we hope for what we do not yet have, we wait for it patiently...* *28 And we know that in all things God works for the good of those who love Him, who[i] have been called according to His purpose...* *31 What, then, shall we say in response to these things? If God is for us, who can be against us?* *35 Who shall separate us from the love of Christ? Shall trouble or hardship or persecution or famine or nakedness or danger or sword?* *37 No, in all these things we are more than conquerors through Him who loved us.* *38 For I am convinced that neither death nor*

life, neither angels nor demons,[k] neither the
present nor the future, nor any powers, [39] neither
height nor depth, nor anything else in all creation,
will be able to separate us from the love of
God that is in Christ Jesus our Lord."

Yes God's promises are true. My entire family was
back together again, and almost complete.

Chapter 3
Set Apart at Birth

"Before I formed you in the womb I knew you, before you were born I set you apart; I appointed you..."
Jeremiah 1:5

I had always wanted to be a nurse. Now that my children were with me, my husband by my side, and him acquiring a job at Sears in the parts department, we were finally settled. This seemed like an opportune time to check out the prospect of nursing as a career. All this time I had been working as a nurse's aide.

In checking out my options I was informed that I had to be a landed immigrant for one year to apply and get accepted into the registered nursing (RN) program and six months for the registered practical nursing (RPN) program. I really wanted to be a RN. However because I did not meet the criteria, I decide to apply to the RPN program.

I soon did just that and was accepted into the RPN program, which would last 9 months. All I had to do was a medical examination before being accepted into the program. One of the criteria was that I could not be pregnant. I did not feel any need for concern, because it was obvious to me that I was not pregnant. It was perfect timing to advance my career. At least that was my thinking until I got back my pregnancy test. I almost told the doctor it can't be and perhaps I needed to repeat the test. I admit I was in a bit of shock. There goes my chance to pursue nursing. I broke down in tears in the doctor's office. "What's wrong," he asked? I told him about the requirements for school entrance. "Oh, I can help you with that," he responded, "you could have an abortion, it's early enough."

I boldly responded, "Doctor that's not an option," and dashed out of his office. I did not see him again until three months later. I went home and told my husband about my dilemma and we prayed about the matter for God's will to be done. The next day I called up the nursing director and made an appointment to meet with her, before the test result got to her. I told her my situation. She said "Well you are taking a big chance, if you take too much time out from classes it will mean you have to drop out of the program and start all over again. Our no pregnancy admission is because of our rigid regulation on absences." I said to her "if you admit me in the program, I will take that chance." I left her presence thanking Lord.

Getting through this program however was not without some challenges. I started school in January 1975 and after a few weeks I started to experience morning sickness. I consoled myself that after three months it would get better but somehow it lasted longer than it had ever been. Somehow God gave me the strength to persist and not give into my feelings.

The real challenge came when one day I ended up in the hospital with abdominal cramps which appeared like contractions. I had to be placed on bed rest. I prayed, "Lord, you have brought me this far and I understand you are in control, but please let me finish this program, and I will not fail to give you glory." When I finished that prayer I had the assurance that God had heard and answered. I still had three weeks to complete my studies and final exams to write. I was in the hospital for a week. I decided to call the school and speak with the director of nursing. She was very understanding and told me that my attendance record was so good, I need not to worry. I only needed to be there to write my final exams. I held up my hands in praise and thanksgiving to God. So often we ask God for deliverance in our trial but we often forget to thank Him and give Him praise. I immediately called my husband and asked him to bring a few of my books and I started to study for my exams in the hospital. *"In my distress I cried unto The Lord and He heard me..."* Psalm120:1.

It was the weekend and I was still in the hospital. I needed to be discharged to be able to write my exams that were scheduled to start on Monday. I could not have the baby yet. By then, the contractions had subsided but the doctor wanted to keep me for a few more days for observation. As I had prayed for and hoped, the doctor discharged me home on bed rest the Monday morning. I went straight to the school and wrote two of my exams before I went home. Fortunately, I was able to complete my final exams with no further setbacks. The final exam was actually written the day prior to my graduation. My colleagues planned a shower at the school for me. They told me, "See you tomorrow at graduation."

I never made it to my graduation or the showers. After I got home I went to bed. My contractions started at 12:30 am on September 12, 1975 my husband rushed me to the hospital. My son Mirthell was born at 5:30 AM, the very day I should have graduated. My diploma was mailed to me with a letter of congratulation. I was able to write my registration a month later and got my license to practice as a registered practical nurse.

Philippians 4:13 says "I can do all things through Christ who strengthens me". We cannot afford to forget the way God has lead us in the past." Jesus promised us "come unto me, all ye that labor and are heavy laden and I will give you rest. Matt 11:28. Notice God does not leave us without any load. The yoke He gives us, is itself a load, but it is purposeful in strengthening our faith rather than tearing it down.

Imagine having two heavy dumbbell weights inside a backpack that you are carrying on your back. The load carried that way may cause harmful strain on your back. That is equivalent to anxiety over our circumstances. But when we go to God He teaches us how to carry the load, challenging us to trust Him while we experience whatever the trial may be through faith in God. Using the imagery, it would be as God taking the weights out of the back pack and placing them in our hands, then instructing us to curl them. In due time our biceps are strengthened and the load becomes light. Whatever trials confronts us, when we trust in God, He will give us not only the strength to endure, but ultimately rest for our souls.

My husband, Carlton was at this time working at sears in Rexdale and also working part-time at Mc-Donald's. It was now time for him to continue his studies into becoming a pastor. We gave up our two bedroom apartment on Weston Rd. and packed our few scanty belongings in a U-Haul hooked up to our old Malibu car and headed for Alberta to Canadian Union College now known as Burman University.

At this time our three children were five, three, and one years old. Carlton was accepted into the Theology program with the expectation when he arrived on campus that a down payment for tuition would be made. We left Toronto with three hundred dollars in hand and no bank account.

We were not aware of credit card those days. If they were around, it was only available to the famous few. One thing was for sure, my husband after getting his last check from work returned his tithe and offering, as was his custom, paid his rent, and asked God to stretch the rest. It took us four days on the road to Alberta, only stopping for catnaps. We had no money for hotels or motel; such luxuries we could not afford. We got to Alberta the evening of the fifth; breathing a sigh of thanksgiving upon arrival. The children, I must say, were good the whole journey.

I got a job in a nursing home the day after I arrived and also ended up working part-time in a hospital in Red Deer as a RPN. Carlton had a job on campus working for the printing press part-time. This was now a certainty that his tuition would now be paid.

God provided in abundance. That first summer holiday, Carlton worked as a literature evangelist selling religious books. He went into every nook and corner of the countryside, suburbs, and farm lands selling Christian books. God blessed his efforts in abundance. He made over $10,000.00 dollars that first summer holiday, and was able to pay off his tuition for the whole year. We were also able to purchase another car so I could drive to work. He bought a little Volkswagen bug, which was good on gas and he loved it.

Being in Alberta was not without challenges, but it was a very rewarding and memorable experience for both of us. We met people that impacted our lives in a positive way. Carlton graduated with a bachelor's degree in theology in April of 1979.

We missed Toronto in the four years we spent in La-Combe, Alberta. After graduation we headed back home. Toronto was now home for us. Getting employment in ministry was very challenging in the late seventies for a black man. We fasted and prayed as a family, and lived with the hope that it would happen. God's purpose prevailed. Carlton was blessed to be hired by the Ontario Conference at the Toronto East church as an assistant pastor, where he graciously served for one year.

"I had fainted, unless I had believed to see the goodness of The Lord in the land of the living."
Psalms 27:13

In 1981 our family packed again, this time for Michigan to Andrews University for Carlton to pursue a Master of Divinity degree at the theological seminary. At this time, I applied to the nursing program where I decided to further my studies. Carlton completed his degree at Andrews University and graduated in 1984. He then had to do some practical field work in Chicago for three months.

I was not able to continue my studies at Andrews University because my dad took seriously ill. As a result of this, I had to withdraw from the program to visit my dad in Jamaica. By this time, I was learning to accept my disappointments as God's appointments, so I patiently rest in Him.

A few months upon return to the U.S. my dad succumbed to his illness and died. My husband and I had to attend the funeral. This was a very trying and difficult time for us. We had no money to go to the funeral. We could not afford to take our three children and would need to leave them with an adult. The student body came to our aid when they heard of our dilemma. They collected some funds and gave us a monetary gift in the sum of $300.00. Two families also offered to keep our children. One family from the church we were attending gave us a monetary gift which was enough to pay for our plane ticket to Jamaica and back.

My father's death was very, very hard to accept. The timing also did not seem right. I missed taking my biology exam and had to drop the registered nursing program. But when I reflected upon the goodness of God and how He opened up opportunities for us and met our desperate need, I could only count my blessings. Despite the setbacks God has lead, God has comforted, God has prospered, God has blessed. This has truly been a journey of faith.

David says, *"Bless the Lord, o my soul: and all that is within me, bless His holy name. Bless the Lord O my soul, and forget not all his benefits"* Psalm 103:1-2. I must also mention that my father who was a devout Catholic and a chain smoker, one year before his diagnosis with lung cancer, gave his heart to God. He had given up smoking, drinking alcohol, and was baptized before he died.

Although he succumbed to this sickness, it gave me peace of mind knowing that my dad gave his heart to God before he died. This was always the prayer of my heart. My dad's death brought so much pain and sadness that I had to receive counseling to help me cope. After having received counseling I was able to look at my pain of loss from God's perspective and was able to find peace.

Upon Carlton completing his field work, we could finally breathe a sigh of relief. He was finished and we were on our way back to Ontario, Canada. He was placed as an assistant pastor at the Toronto West church.

I continued to work alongside my husband in ministry and cared for our children. I also considered going back to work as a RPN. I did not however feel complete in this role, so I proceeded to check my options on how I could continue my studies in becoming a registered nurse.

I eventually was successful in being accepted to George Brown College. I also sent out applications to different hospitals and nursing homes for employment in nursing. The first place that responded to my application was Riverdale hospital where I previously worked. I was desperate for a job so I was interviewed and offered a position, which I accepted. I truly felt God's leading and guidance in my life. Life became very busy, but we were off to a good start.

I started George Brown College with great optimism and looked forward to graduating in three years. I also continued to work part-time. By now, all three children were in church school and the tuition for them was costly. I had to be very organized to cope with school, work, household chores, and family life.

My husband was a great support to me in this endeavor. I could not have made it without him. Carlton drove me to classes most mornings and to clinical practice, especially when I had to get there for 6:30 am.

He would stay up with me in the late hours of the night when I had to complete my nursing care plans. I give thanks to God for having placed him in my life. Carlton was truly a gift from God. We both supported each other in everything that was meaningful and fulfilling to us both. We gave first priority to anything that would be in the best interest of our family and for the cause of God.

Completing my nursing studies at George Brown College was not without challenges and setbacks. In fact I failed my pediatric clinical rotation and had to repeat it. Nevertheless, I graduated from George Brown College in 1988. I wrote my license a few months after and was successful in passing.

It was truly a delight to support my husband in ministry as I affirmed him and prayed for him when the going got tough, and the challenges of ministry seemed overwhelming. One of the greatest challenges of ministry, particularly for myself and the children, was instability. Every three to five years my husband would be transferred to a new district. Sometimes this required changing our place of residence. This was especially burdensome for our children, as it was difficult to make friends and keep them. This in itself has taught them to put self aside, and to learn the gift of sacrifice. If you marry a man or woman of God that you are not prepared to share with the people and with God, then I would say marrying a pastor is a big mistake. However, if this is your experience I would encourage you to seek God's divine wisdom in how He can use you to be a blessing to your partner that is   called   to   ministry.

I personally stepped out of the way and allowed God and the Holy Spirit to use the man He blessed me with to bring honor and glory to His name. Ministry also brought a lot of satisfaction especially when the congregation showed appreciation for your service. We felt very happy as a family when we were appreciated but sad when we were misunderstood. These are the times when we would go to God in prayer, thank Him for the good times and prayed for misunderstandings to be made clear.

Ministry can be very lonely for the wife of pastors especially if you do not have any outside interests, career etc. You feel lonely even in the congregation, and it's often no different for the pastor himself. Unlike the pastor's wife, the pastor can those emotions by keeping himself busy with church work. Nevertheless, there was no other calling that brought meaning and satisfaction to my husband as ministry. He worked hard at it and I thank God I supported him in fulfilling his dream in this life. I stood by his side many times not because I felt like it, because sometimes I didn't. I stood by his side not because I loved him, and only God knows how much I did. I stood by his side because of the grace of God. God extends grace to me over and over again throughout my life time, when I don't even deserve it.

God gave me the wisdom to extend grace to my husband and the holy calling He extended to him. God had also chosen me to be by his side and to support him despite the challenges of ministry.

"And He said unto me, my grace is sufficient for thee: for my strength is made perfect in weakness, most gladly therefore will I rather glory in my infirmities that the power of Christ may rest upon

me. Therefore I take pleasure in infirmities, in
reproaches, in necessities, in persecutions, in
distresses for Christ sake: for when I am weak,
then am I strong."
2 Corinthians 12:9-10

It was while pastoring in his sixth church that I received the devastating news. I had gone to see my family doctor to get my yearly physical done. In the past I would shy away from having a Pap smear to check my cervix, however this time I was compelled to do so because I was experiencing some discomfort. My test result came back positive and I was referred to a gynecologist for further tests. Upon examination it was discovered that I had endometriosis and cancer of the cervix.

This was frightening for me as a young mother of 37 years old and with three children who were sixteen, fourteen and twelve years old. My father had died from lung cancer, so the question that confronted me was, will this be my fate also? I wanted to see my children at least get through college and even to be at their wedding to give my blessing. I prayed and prayed to God for His intervention and healing. Thanks be to God, the long and short is the cancerous growth was found early and was removed.

It has been twenty nine years since this incident occurred. God indeed has been merciful in answer to my prayer. Must I forget the way The Lord has lead me in the past? No I cannot forget. We must trust God at His word and hold on to His promises, that He will see us through every trial and suffering that we are faced with. God is always faithful, I am the one that over and over again is weak in faith.

Each time I am faced with another trial I would tell God, "If you get me through this one I will never doubt you again!" But is it because I doubt that God will answer? Or is it more that I am impatient and want God to answer now, or on my terms? May be both.

We must understand that God is faithful to resolve our difficulties in His time. We may want Him to act sooner, but only He knows the perfect time to accomplish His purposes. Yes God healed me, nevertheless, if God had chosen to do otherwise I would still be blessed. Why? Because blessings come in accepting God's will and plan for our lives. We should allow our suffering to lead us to a greater intimacy with Christ, thus preparing us for heaven to live with Him.

"Humble yourselves therefore under the mighty hand of God, that He may exalt you in due time, casting all your cares upon Him for He cares for you".
1 Peter 5:6-7

Through it all I could always rely on my husband for support. My husband and I were each other's best friend on earth, and what made it so sweet was that we both made Jesus our best friend also. This made all the difference during our ups and downs, but in reflection I now realize that this was actually our time of ups. It was our time of partnership and intimacy. It was our time of accomplishments fulfilled. It was our time of family being complete and together. It was our time of the dream being fulfilled.

The word of the Lord came to me, saying,
5 "Before I formed you in the womb I
knew[a] you, before you were born I set you
apart; I appointed you as a prophet to the
nations."6 "Alas, Sovereign Lord," I said, "I do
not know how to speak; I am too young." 7 But
the Lord said to me, "Do not say, 'I am too
young.' You must go to everyone I send you to and
say whatever I command you. 8 Do not be
afraid of them, for I am with you and will
rescue you," declares the Lord. 9 Then
the Lord reached out his hand and touched my
mouth and said to me, "I have put my words in
your mouth. 10 See, today I appoint you over
nations and kingdoms to uproot and tear down, to
destroy and overthrow, to build and to plant."
Jeremiah 1:4-9

I believe that God gives us dreams and then fulfills those dreams. As a young girl I began to sense my divine purpose, before it was even remotely a possibility. Then I watched as God fulfilled the dream right before my eyes. My husband didn't even know that I was dreaming of marrying a pastor, and he never even thought of becoming a pastor when we married, until God reveal that plan to him later. While I dreamed of being a nurse I never could have imagined how God would make it possible, but He did!

In reflection I have enjoyed being a nurse for over 30 years and blessed to retire as a Registered Nurse in October 2014. I was also blessed to support my husband for over 30 years of pastoral ministry.

Never give up on the dreams and purpose God has given you. Hard times will come to test your faith. You may even doubt, but great is His faithfulness towards you. In the hardest of times if you stop and listen, you will hear God's still quiet voice assure you with this promise:

For I know the plans I have for you," declares the LORD, "plans to prosper you and not to harm you, plans to give you hope and a future. [12] Then you will call on me and come and pray to me, and I will listen to you. [13] You will seek me and find me when you seek me with all your heart.
Jeremiah 29:11-13

Chapter 4
Joy Comes in the Mourning

"Blessed are those who mourn, for they will be comforted."
Matthew 5:4

Never in my wildest dreams would I ever have imagined this to be the fate of my son. I had envisioned him becoming an adult with a career, and getting married with children of his own. However this was not to be. Life is filled with experiences some pleasant and some disappointing ones. Regardless of the experience, we need to continue to trust God's loving providence. Since we cannot see what God sees, the alternative is to keep our eyes on God. As we look to Him rather than looking at our circumstances we can be at peace. Isaiah 26:3 says *"thou wilt keep him in perfect peace whose mind is stayed on thee."*

In 1992 my eldest son Pedro became mentally ill. Pedro grew up as a healthy, happy, caring, and well-built young man. In his early childhood and early teens he manifested no signs and symptoms of mental illness. My first indication that something was wrong was at age 17. Friday evening was a high time for us in the Mitchell home. At sunset every Friday we would come together as a family for our special worship service in thanksgiving to God. There was a time when my son would be actively involved in leading our worship service. Now it was the total opposite. Pedro would be rushing to leave the house on a Friday evening and showed a disinterest in any spiritual activity or connection.

When he would attend family worship he would literally make our worship time miserable, often rushing us through it. It was as though he was becoming demon possessed. As time progressed and I became more aware of the situation I got a hunch that he may have been trying drugs, but he denied it. To this date this was not proven, but he did admit sometime later that he was visiting strip clubs. This was where he and some of his friends would hang out on Friday nights.

This was just heartbreaking for me and my husband. It was like a nightmare and we were concerned that this would have a negative influence on our younger children. This behavior persisted for a while. After we prayerfully talked to him about the danger of visiting these kinds of places he stopped.

I recall him coming home from school one day while attending community college. He was manifesting a strange behavior. However, he went to his room and I was unable to talk to him as he would not allow me in. As a young adult and wanting to respect his privacy I did not force my way in. Pedro's condition worsened as he got older. He started several colleges in pursuit of a career but was never able to complete as he would become ill before the semester finished.

It was difficult for the doctors to specify exactly what his diagnosis was, as at times he manifested symptoms of manic depression and bipolar disorder. He was very noncompliant with taking his medication, sometimes taking only a half of a tablet or not taking it at all. Because of his non-compliance his illness was difficult to treat resulting in relapse.

One day while my husband was conducting a very special event at the church, Pedro had an emotional outburst that was disturbing to the service. Fortunately, I was able to quietly take him out and took him home. That evening I had to call 911 and he eventually had to be restrained chemically and ended up staying overnight at the hospital.

During these times of uncertainty our family had to make several adjustments to be able to cope with these challenging moments. It was very heart breaking for all of us seeing him this way. Pedro's behavior affected my younger son Mirthell, so much so that he spent most of his time sleeping over at his best friend's house. I realized how difficult it was for him seeing his older brother with such a drastic change in personality and often so difficult to relate to.

We prayed and prayed but God seemed silent to our cry. Instead of my son getting better, his condition worsened. It was also very difficult for my daughter Rosia. She no doubt went through a lot in her mind and had questions that we as parents could not answer. At this time we ourselves had questions that to this date I am unable to answer. What may have happened in his childhood that may have triggered mental illness? Did we miss picking up something earlier in his development years that could have helped him receive early treatment? What could I have done better as a mother?

Parents tend toward attributing personal responsibility for their children's success. I have actually heard parents brag about their children's success, taking credit for it all. Do they do the same when things don't turn out quite so right?

My husband and I were not perfect parents by no means, but we always turned to God in the good and the bad times. Rather than wallowing in guilt we turned our children over to God. Rather than swelling up with pride we gave thanks for all He has done in them and through them.

I have heard some people say, it would be better not to have children, I disagree. What I will say is despite the frustration and challenges I have had in raising my children, they have all been a blessing in my life. My husband has expressed the same sentiments.

Unless the Lord builds the house,
those who build it labor in vain…

3 Behold, children are a heritage from the Lord,
the fruit of the womb a reward...
5 Blessed is the man
who fills his quiver with them!
Psalms 127:1, 3, 5

No matter how challenging your children are never stop reflecting the unconditional love of Christ in your speech, attitude, and interactions. Despite what your eyes see or what your heart feels, show them Christ not self, reveal the spirit not the flesh. Our children must come to see Christ in us; the very same Jesus that *"while we were yet sinners, Christ died for us." Romans 5:8.*

Pedro had once again dropped out of college. He had once again taken ill and his Dad had to travel to Alberta where he was attending school to take him home to Toronto for medical attention. He was in the mental health center for almost six weeks but got well enough to return home. We continued to intercede in prayer for healing. We were so happy to see him in a state of wellness and in good spirit to be able to attend his younger brother, Mirthell's wedding in Huntsville, Alabama on December 20, 1998.

This was a great time of celebration, and family togetherness. My sister was there from England and other family members all travelled to the wedding of our son. Pedro remained stable and well. We had a great time at the wedding. Pedro gave a speech at the wedding on his brother's behalf. No one would have known that he suffered from any kind of mental incapacity. We were thankful we were all together and all went well. Even traveling back to Toronto was so much fun, as we all talked, laughed, and reflected as a family.

Pedro was now living at home and he remained stable for a while. Later he started to express interest in returning to college to continue to pursue his career. We did not want to encourage him to do so, because the stress of studies always seemed to trigger off a relapse in his illness. Two months after the wedding, Pedro was beginning to get restless and requesting money to register for college.

It was February 4, 1999. The day before I had left my son at home for work, he had told me that he was going to visit his doctor to adjust his medication. Whatever symptoms Pedro was experiencing that day, he kept it to himself. Pedro knew he was sick but he wanted to be autonomous. I imagine he must have thought adjusting the drugs would help him cope. I had given him fresh linen to make his bed, also money to buy a packet of tokens for travel. My husband and I left for work as we had many other mornings. Pedro was at home with his grandmother, and he seemed in good spirits; little did we know that day would end with my son being history.

We had heard that just prior to heading towards the platform where the trains arrived, Pedro bought his transportation fare for the month. Ironically, he would not need it, for today would be his final destination. Pedro, my loving son, never made it back home.

Hiding behind a pillar, he seemed to onlookers paranoid. But of what? He seemed to be highly anxious to board the oncoming train? But running away from what? Perhaps right there in that subway station, he had succumbed to the voices that plagued him since being stricken with mental illness. We believe that Pedro was hit by the same train he so desperately was hoping to get on.

My husband had just returned home at one in the afternoon, when there was a knock on the door. He opened the door to the grim news from a police officer that our son was hit and killed by the subway train. I was at work on the evening shift. The police officer, not wanting him to travel alone, was kind to drive behind my husband, accompanying him to my work place to bring me the news. Needless to say, I felt numb and in shock.

For weeks to follow this made no sense to me. When the sun went down, I would lay in bed, tossing and turning trying to fall asleep. Maybe I would awaken from this nightmare. Only to wake up with the rising of the sun, forced to live out this bad dream. I did not believe this really happened until I viewed my son's body in the funeral home. I called him by name and touched him and told him son, I know you did not do this in your right frame of mind. It was very hard to stand there and look at his body that was obviously put back together.

A lump came to my throat which hurt and would not go away. How could this be happening? Pedro loved life, he loved his family, and he loved the Lord. His journal that he left behind testified of this. I knew that this was not his doing, but rather a result of the voices that constantly plagued him. He had recently recommitted his life to God and had left that past life behind him. This was why I could not make sense of it. I was in disbelief. So many questions plagued my mind, for which I had no answer. Only God would have the answer to these questions.

Just after my son's funeral my husband and I left for Jamaica to visit my father-in-law. This was actually meant to be a little getaway from the tragic death of my son. We planned to spend a night at a good friend of his in Westmoreland, then she would take us to Kingston where my father-in-law resides. My husband was asked to preach at his friend's church on Saturday and we would leave to see his father on Sunday. My husband called his dad but was unable to speak with him, he however left a message that we would see him the Sunday. Thanks be to an all wise God that our future and the future of our loved ones is hidden from us. But the future does not belong to us, it belongs to God alone.

Friday my husband and I drove into the city square to shop around a bit. Upon returning to our friend's place, we saw that she had the first elder of her church visiting. As I walked in I noticed that her expression had changed. She then asked my husband, "Pastor, when last have you read the book of Job?" The question was barely out of her mouth when I responded, "What happened? Is my mother ok? Are my children ok?" She said yes. So I ask again what has happened? After all we are there to visit his dad, he has to be ok. Finally I caught on, "Pastor, when last did you read the book of Job?" I asked her again, "What is happening, please tell us what it is!" She hesitated but rather asked the elder visiting to pray. She then broke the news, "Pastor your father died this morning".

Immediately, my husband left us without any response regarding this news. He locked himself in the bathroom and I could not get in to be with him. After trying to ask him to open the door, I decided to give him time alone. I then took some time to pray by myself. I thank God that she had decided to call the elder over to pray with us before she broke the news. My husband was in the bathroom for what seemed like an hour. I tried to get him to open the door, but the Holy Spirit said leave him and so I kept praying for him. Thank God he was strengthened. I don't know how he did it, but God empowered him to preach a powerful message the following day Saturday. Early Sunday morning our friend took us to my father-in-law's home.

My husband never saw his father alive on his visit to Jamaica. It was a sad occasion for us. It was just not to be. Some things just do not make sense; in this world, unseen forces are continually at work against us. Here we are, we just buried our son, and we went to Jamaica on a getaway trip to reflect and to be with family members, only to be faced with another significant loss of his father.

In the deepest trials of life we often have no earthly options but to fall into the loving arms of God for comfort. If God does not comfort we cannot be comforted. When God comes alongside you in your suffering and ministers to your hurting heart you will find healing. I believe God did just that, especially to my husband. That despite his pain and the sad news, he was still able to stand strong and delivered the good news of the spoken word to a waiting church. I thank God for that hope we have in Christ.

"If in this life only we have hope in Christ, we are all men most miserable. But now is Christ risen from the dead, and become the first fruits of them that slept. For since by man came death, by man came also the resurrection of the dead."
1 Corinthians 15:19-21

I understand that my father-in-law's wish, was for us to get there and to explain to him how his grandson had died. It was never meant to be.

I was hurting, my husband was hurting, and my children were hurting. Where is God in all of this? Right there where He has always been. There is no need for me to even ask that question. God has shown me over and over again.

"For My thoughts are not your thoughts, neither are your ways My ways, saith the Lord. For as the heavens are higher than the earth, so are My ways higher than your ways and My thoughts than your thoughts."
Isaiah 55:8

We spent three weeks in Jamaica and buried our father before we returned to Canada. Over and over again, I asked my husband why would God allow your father to die before we saw him and could speak with him. He would say to me, "God is perfect in His ways. Stop trying to figure God out!" We can't figure God out, and that's why God has told us not even to try.

I prayed and got enough courage to remind myself that I am a child of God and I must trust God at His word. I was reminded *"in everything give thanks: for this is the will of God in Christ Jesus concerning you..."* 1 Thessalonians 5:18. Then must I trust God and thank Him for only the things that seem pleasing and good to me? Although I did not seem ready to accept this profound truth from God's word, I kept repeating it, and kept praying and asking God to help me believe it.

Night after night I went to bed agonizing with God and seeking an answer from Him as to why my son died in this way. The question as to whether he may have deliberately took his own life was a pressing one. We all searched his room but found nothing except his journal that acknowledged God and his trust in God. This gave me some hope, but not completely. I lived my life in pain for many months to follow.

This particular night, I knelt and prayed and asked God for an answer. I promised that if He answered me, I promised to dry my tears and would use this tragic and painful experience to give glory to Him. I retired to bed as usual and soon fell asleep. Early in the morning at around three o'clock I was awakened by a gentle touch and a voice that said hymn 310. I was conscious but still very sleepy so I fell off to sleep again with the mindset to read that hymn in the morning. I dozed off and felt another touch and the same voice saying hymn 310. This time I got out of bed and took my hymnal and read. I broke down in tears after reading those words. It was as though God was talking to me in the words of that hymn.

I had to awaken my husband from sleep and share with him the words from that hymn, especially the

2nd stanza! I continue to give thanks to God who would care so much for me that He would answer the cry of my heart in such an awesome way. What was so remarkable about it was that I had never seen that hymn before! The midnight message has cleared up all doubt in my mind that God loves and cares for me and He answers prayers.

HYMN 510
SDA HYMNAL

If you but trust in God to guide you and place your confidence in Him,
You'll find Him always there beside you to give you hope and strength within.
For those who trust God's changeless love build on the rock that will not move.

What gain is there in futile weeping, in helpless anger and distress?
If you are in His care and keeping, in sorrow will He love you less?
For He who took for you a cross will bring you safe through every loss

In patient trust await His leisure in cheerful hope, with heart content
To take whatever your fathers pleasure and all discerning love have sent;

Doubt not your in most wants are known To
Him who chose you for His own.

Sing, pray and keep His ways unswerving,
offer your service faithfully,
and trust His word; though undeserving, you'll
find His promise true to be. God never will
forsake in need the soul that trust in Him
indeed.

Jesus promises us in Matthew 5:4, *"Blessed are those who mourn, for they will be comforted..."* Like David who cried out to God in Psalms 6:8 "collect my tears in your bottle." Likewise, I know God heard my cry, saw my tears, and was moved to comfort me.

The bible says "Weeping may endure for a night, but joy *cometh* in the morning." Psalms 30:5. Some look at this text to mean that the joy promised in this text refers to a future fulfillment, such as the day when Jesus returns and wipes every tear from our eyes. While it is true that when Jesus comes the old things will pass away, this does not mean we cannot experience God's healing power from grief and loss. *"Blessed are those who mourn for they will be comforted"* is a present promise; meaning you may be in grief and weep today but God's joy can also be experienced today if you lean on Him in your mourning. This is why I now say "Weeping may endure for a night, but joy *cometh* in the m-o-u-r-n-i-n-g." So go ahead don't hold back, share your pain and grief with God. He wants to comfort you.

I have never been the same since this revelation in answer to my prayer. My burden had been lifted and I felt at peace. I have since used this hymn as a source of encouragement in reminding me that God is with me despite the challenges I face from day to day. I have since been able to talk freely without any compunction about my son's illness and death, and even about how he died. I have been able to reach out to others who have had near to similar experiences of illness and loss. Praise be to God, for His love and mercy extended towards me in answer to my cry.

Let's take time to show appreciation for one another. Let's give God first place in our lives. Let's testify of His love for us. God's answer to my prayer has made a lasting impact on my life. It has drawn me so close to Him that all I can say over and over again, is God you are awesome! Just awesome! Thank you for loving me. I commit to serve you by God's grace for the rest of my life.

Chapter 5
MAKE ME OR BREAK ME

*"Behold, I have refined thee, but not with silver;
I have chosen thee in the furnace of affliction."*
Isaiah 48:10

One of the things I looked forward to doing, was to go into old age with my husband. We would often talk about growing old together. When we would see an elderly couple walking and holding hands, he would comment, "That's us when we are in our eighties." At that moment, it was just a frivolous wish, an earthly desire. Nothing is wrong with that desire because we enjoyed being with each other and having long life is indeed a blessing. However, the Lord my shepherd had a better plan in mind. Our plans do not always fall into God's scheme of things because our plans are usually based on earthly desires.

When we approach life from a self-centered perspective and not the plan that God has for us, sometimes we become confused, if not frustrated, about the change of events in our lives. This does not mean that God does not want for us to live happy and fulfilled lives. For He is the same God who declared in 3 John 2:2

"Beloved, I wish above all things that thou may prosper and be in good health, even as thy soul prosper."

God also longs to develop a closer relationship with us, this is why in Luke 12:31 Jesus says *"But rather seek ye first the Kingdom of God; and all these things shall be added unto you"*. When God formed us in our mother's womb he had every plan laid out just right for us. We just need to trust Him that all our earthly needs will be supplied just right. Our food, clothing, shelter, and length of our days are all in His omnipotent hands. What God wants for us is to know His perspective, His desires, and His perfect plan for our lives. He is looking for partners to obey Him and His instructions to us.

Allow me to say that God is more interested in developing a relationship with us and saving us than our individual comfort in this life. Why am I saying all of this? We simple do not know the future, we need to let go of our lives and let God have full and complete control.

On January 30, 2000, my husband and I were getting ready to leave the house. It was his fiftieth birthday and we were going to Mother Tucker's restaurant to celebrate. The telephone rang and he answered it. It was the doctor's office calling for him to come in the next day for an urgent prostate test result. He had just had a PSA done for the first time, a week or so prior to receiving this call. What now Lord! I said in my mind, doctors offices don't usually call unless a test result is abnormal.

The following morning I accompanied him to see the urologist. The test result showed a PSA reading of 11.8. The normal reading should have been less than 4.0. The urologist informed him that it was crucial for him to do surgery as soon as possible. Surgery was planned immediately and the prostate successfully removed effectually getting rid of the cancer. Unfortunately some of the lymph node was involved. Chemotherapy was recommended but Mitch which I affectionately called him, refused, because of the known fact that chemo also damages good cell and there is no guarantee that it cures cancer. Every treatment was prayerfully considered. Mitch continued with the hormone treatment he was receiving, even though this also carried its own side effects and discomfort.

One of the biggest setbacks and difficulty my husband faced was scar tissue from the surgery. This scar tissue would form a keloid and would block off his passageway making it difficult for him to urinate. My husband literally had to visit the hospital every two to three months to clear this passage way so he could urinate freely. Each time he had to wear a catheter for six to eight weeks after this procedure. This was often uncomfortable for him, but he did not let this discomfort get in the way of performing his pastoral duties. He looked forward to when he could remove the catheter and appreciate the freedom of passing his urine in a normal way. We prayed that the scar tissue would get better but it only got worse.

Let me back up a bit. The doctor had told Mitch that if he didn't do the surgery he would only have a year or less to live. The cancer was termed aggressive because he was only 50 years of age when he was diagnosed. His hormones apparently also played a major factor in the spread of the disease. I was frightened by this prognosis and the uncertainty of what could be.

A few weeks after Mitch's diagnosis, I can recall my daughter-in-law asking me, "mom how do you feel about dad's illness?" In response I said to her, "Rita I believe God can and will heal my husband. I am asking God for at least 10 more years with my husband and to prepare me emotionally and physically for what will be." Ten years seemed long compared to one year if he had refused surgery. The dialogue with my new daughter continued, God bless her, she gave me food for thought and a greater desire to persevere in prayer. She asked me, "Mom, what if ten years is not a part of God's plan? What if He gives you the ten years, you might be disappointed that you did not have ten more years." I said to her, "Rita, I love my God. I will accept whatever God's plan is for me. Whether one year or ten years, but I am sure that God will give us at least

10 more years together." I said it with assurance and I believed it with all my heart.

Coping with my husband's illness was quite a challenge, but God gave me the strength as I persevered in prayer. I thank God for my church family, friends and family members who also interceded on his behalf. I also thank God for my experience as a registered nurse which allowed me to cope and care for him with confidence.

Let me remind you here that from the day of his surgery his life had not been completely normal. There was always an interruption every six to eight weeks where the doctor had to clear the scar tissue and reinsert a new catheter.

My worst nightmare was to be realized one night on my trip with him to the hospital. We had to go to the emergency department again, but this time things did not go as well as other times. He was not wearing a catheter then and he was totally blocked and unable to urinate even a trickle. You could tell he was in severe discomfort. The urologist on-call did not want to do the necessary procedure, so he telephoned for my husband's urologist to come to the hospital. Thank God he was at home and he responded to the call.

I had a gut feeling that this time the procedure would not go as smoothly. It was 1:00 o'clock in the morning as I waited while my husband was transported to the operating room. I felt alone and low in spirit. I called out to God from the bottom of my soul. I needed to be comforted. I paced the floor from one corner of the hospital waiting area to the next with no one in sight until my legs became wobbly.

Finally the door opened and his doctor came with the news. Not good he said, the scar tissue was very hard to remove and while operating the scope broke off. He asked for my permission to insert a permanent supra pubic catheter instead of the temporary removable Foley catheter. This was my biggest fear, just how would my husband accept this altered self-image?

After the doctor left, I cried, "Oh Jesus, please help me cope!" I thank God that my husband was still alive. I dashed outside the hospital for some fresh air. I became nauseated and started to throw up. I just needed someone to hug me tight and even to pray with me. There was no human touch around and I felt so alone. By then it was about 3:00 am in the morning and I didn't want to wakeup Clover, my sister-in-law, or my children. Finally, I decided to call Clover anyway and told her what had happened. After talking with her I felt better.

The insertion of the supra pubic catheter was successful, and my husband remained in the hospital for three weeks before he was released home. Mitch had to get adjusted to having the supra pubic catheter, but he was a real trooper and mastered the skill of managing this new adjustment with his care. He also adjusted readily to this altered self-image. My husband lived with this new normalcy for the next two years.

In 2009 the cancer returned and he was given less than one year to live. This time he agreed to take radiation for the purpose of pain management. He was very accepting of the prognosis. In December of 2009, although his condition was weak and he needed a wheel chair for traveling, I accompanied him to Jamaica as this was his wish to visit for the last time to connect with his siblings.

Although in pain, he enjoyed every moment of it, especially, when the pain was lessened. During his short stay he witnessed and encouraged others to come to know God. During these last months we spent every moment we could with each other in very meaningful ways. About eight weeks before his death, he still had some strength so we went to the park in Brampton. We sat on a bench in the park and admired the beautiful flowers. We talked about any and everything and reflected on the life we spent together. At one time there was silence and I got closer to him. His thoughts seemed far off. I looked at him and asked, "Honey, what is your biggest fear?" He looked at me and said with tears streaming down his cheeks "My biggest fear is to die and leave you behind and alone." This was the first time I have seen my husband cry. I responded truthfully, "This was my biggest fear also, to watch you die and to be left behind." Then he said to me, "I am sorry honey…If you knew I would leave you so early would you have married me?" I told him, "I would have married you a thousand times over." The conversation continued into a reminder of what death was all about, a reminder of it being only a sleep, and we comforted ourselves with God's promise.

"Marvel not at this: for the hour is coming, in which all that are in the graves shall hear his voice, [29] and shall come forth; they that have done good, unto the resurrection of life; and they that have done evil, unto the resurrection of damnation."
John 5:28-29

We promised each other to remain faithful until Jesus comes or until we die. We hugged each other and felt at peace. This was our last meaningful conversation. The last few weeks of his condition had deteriorated and he could not leave the house. He was mostly from bed to the chair. He was in severe pain and spent much of his time sleeping to conserve energy. It was painful for me to see him suffering and it was painful to know he was leaving me.

The fact that God answered my prayer and gave me the ten years and no less that I had asked for meant much to me. This was an indication that God listens and that He cares. He could have even given me an additional 1 more year to reach our milestone 40th year anniversary but God knows my heart and the sincerity of my prayer 10 years back. He knew it would be more meaningful for me to know that my God heard my prayers and sympathized with my human desires, than to even give me one more year with my husband. In answering my prayer of ten years, it was affirming and it drew me closer to Him. This has helped me to develop a more trusting relationship with my God.

My husband was diagnosed on January 30, 2000 and died March 5, 2010. I knew he was slipping away when he stopped speaking on Wednesday. He stopped eating and was losing a lot of energy. All day Thursday he lay in bed. It was Friday, however, at sunset that he closed his eyes and took his last breathe. He died in the comfort of his own home with his family members, friends and colleagues in ministry by his side.

"This is the word that came to Jeremiah from the LORD: ² "Go down to the potter's house, and there I will give you my message." ³ So I went down to the potter's house, and I saw him working at the wheel. ⁴ But the pot he was shaping from the clay was marred in his hands; so the potter formed it into another pot, shaping it as seemed best to him."
Jeremiah 18:1-4

The devil wants us to focus on our brokenness. He might have thought my husband's death would be the final tragedy to break me. But to be broken in the hands of the Potter is different than to simply be broken. In the Potter's hands He often breaks us to remake us. Isaiah 48:10 says, *"Behold, I have refined thee, but not with silver; I have chosen thee in the furnace of affliction."*

Parting was difficult. Many years ago I would often say, I don't know what I would do if my husband died before me. But experiencing it for myself, I can assure you, with God by your side, when the time comes *"You can do all things through Christ who strengthens you."* Philippians 4:13.

God has been very merciful to me and very gracious. He is a timely God and He prepared me in every way to be able to cope with my husband's death. You see our God knows us more than we know ourselves. He knows what each of His children can handle, and I believe He would only allow certain situations that best work with our personality. His desire in everything is always to draw us closer to Him.

There will never be a perfect timing for any of our loved ones to leave this earth or even in facing our own death. We just have to learn to trust God. Though we may not understand His actions we can trust His heart.

I thank God that He actually gave me the strength to embrace what He has allowed in my life. In all of this I never once felt anger against God. I have shed many tears. I have even questioned God when in my grief. When the temptation of fear came upon me to worry about the future I chose instead to pray. Each time I chose to pray I would rise from my knees with a feeling of peace.

"Woe to the one who quarrels with his Maker-- An earthenware vessel among the vessels of earth! Will the clay say to the potter, 'What are you doing?' Or the thing you are making say, 'He has no hands'?"
Isaiah 45:9

I thank God that I can sincerely say my husband's illness and subsequent death has impacted my life in a more positive way than negative. It has drawn me closer to God. He has shown me in many ways that he loves me and He will take care of me. Thanks be to God this trial did not break me but made me a stronger individual in Christ.

"And we know that all things work together for good to them that love God, to them who are the called according to [his] purpose"
Romans 8:28.

Chapter 6
The God in My Afflictions

"Come to me, all you who are weary and burdened, and I will give you rest. [29] Take my yoke upon you and learn from me, for I am gentle and humble in heart, and you will find rest for your souls. [30] For my yoke is easy and my burden is light."
Matthew 11:28-30

I was sitting in the front row of the church. I could see his face, once full and healthy looking, now emaciated from the effect of the terrible disease of cancer.

It was time to close the casket. It's over now, it's over now *(the music played softly in the background).* Pictures of our life together flashed on the screen. Scenes from our youth, young adult, and midlife displaying some of the most memorable times. At the end of the short sideshow it reset to start over again, set to loop for as long as needed. If only this was the case, that Mitch and I could experience it all over again and again. But it's over now I thought! I will never see the love of my life again. Not in this life anyways.

I was in a church filled with friends and family and well-wishers, but felt alone in my emotions. Please God you have promised to take care of me. I never dreamed my life with him would end this way.

Death was not supposed to be a part of it, but wait a minute! Didn't I say till death do us part? Yes only death could part us. But the wonderful memories of the life we shared will always resonate like yesterday.

Soon the service in the church was over and we were headed to the cemetery where he would be placed in the ground. I literally started to psyche myself up for this. I knew that I would literally pass out if I didn't. I started to focus on heaven and on Jesus' soon return to take His loved ones home. By the time we got to the grave side I did not see or hear what took place. My focus was intensely upon Jesus' return and His call for my husband to come forth. I have that blessed assurance in the word of God.

"For the Lord himself will come down from heaven, with a loud command, with the voice of the archangel and with the trumpet call of God, and the dead in Christ will rise first. [17] After that, we who are still alive and are left will be caught up together with them in the clouds to meet the Lord in the air. And so we will be with the Lord forever.
1 Thessalonians 4:16, 17

God gave me the peace I needed to sustain me at that moment of intense grief. God had shown me in many of my life events, which took place leading up to this time, which He is faithful in answering my prayers. I have learned to claim His promises like in Psalm 54:22 *"Cast thy burden upon the Lord, and He shall sustain thee: He shall never suffer the righteous to be moved."*

There were no more tears left in my eyes. When tears were no longer spilling out, they must have begun turning inward, pouring down into my heart…for my heart was now heavy. However, the great promises of God from His word in that moment began to sustain me and gave me joy within, though my heart was broken.

"They that sow in tears shall reap in joy. He that goeth forth and weepeth, bearing precious seed, shall doubtless come again with rejoicing bringing his sheaves with him."
Psalms 126:5, 6

Believe it or not I was stronger at the gravesite than I expected. I even walked towards the grave and looked in when he was being lowered down. My mind was intensely focused on Jesus' soon return and calling my husband from the grave to come forth. I thank God for His loving assurance from His word that kept me calm throughout.

Family members were gathered at my home after the funeral. It was a good feeling to have them around. I tried to keep my composure and tried to show appreciation for their presence, but my human emotions got the better of me. I retreated to my room and I cried until every bit of energy seemed drained from my body. I thank God for my sister Gloria who had come to visit from England, she encouraged me to rest awhile, while she entertained family and friends.

My sister stayed with me an additional three weeks after his death. While she was with me, my mind was kept occupied on other things, and we talked about my husband quite a bit. This also helped with my grieving. During the first few weeks I would visit the gravesite every day. This was only a five minute drive from my house. Visiting the gravesite just before I would go to bed at night was also comforting to me.

During the ten years of my husband's illness God had prepared me to be accepting of what His plan for my husband would be. As his condition deteriorated and the pain became more severe and relentless, it was getting harder to see him in this way. I realized then that I had to let go and let God. God in His mercy had prepared me to submit to His will for our lives.

I am grateful to be a child of God, because I know I could not go through this journey of loss all by myself. I needed God to hold me and guide me through those difficult times. I needed to pray without ceasing and to claim and trust His promises, this was my only means of survival.

*"For we have not an high priest which cannot be
touched with the feelings of our infirmities; but
was in all points tempted like as we are, yet
without sin . Let us come boldly unto the throne of
grace, that we may obtain mercy,
and find grace to help in time of need."*
Hebrews 4: 15-16

Quoting scripture and meditating on the word of
God became a way of life for me and still is to this
day. Our only way to find rest in God is to delight
in His word. We cannot allow Satan who is the
author of confusion and adversary of evil on this
earth to steal our joy.

*"There hath no temptation taken you but such as is
common to man; but God is faithful, who will not
suffer you to be tempted above that Ye are able;
but will with the temptation also make a way of
escape , that Ye may be able to bear it."*
1 Corinthians 10:13

You see Mitch was not only my husband, he was
my best friend, my confidant, losing him was like
losing everything. One thing though, that made a
difference, was that we had both given God first
place in our lives. I allowed him to put God first and
he allowed me to put God first. Ultimately we
shared this one all important thing in common,
placing God first in our lives. So when Mitch was
gone, having shared a common love for God was as
though a major part of Mitch was still with me.

Our shared relationship with God is the formula for success in any healthy Christian marriage. Now that Mitch was gone, I continued to draw strength from God, who had now become my main source of strength. I constantly reminded myself, that God is faithful, and that the same God that took me through my son's death will take me through my husband's death.

One Friday evening as the sun was about to set, I went to the gravesite to have my worship. We were accustomed to having a special worship at home together on a Friday evening, in thanksgiving for the Sabbath day of rest.

All seemed to have been going well. I had completed my worship in reading the scripture and praying. The sun had set and I was about to go home. Suddenly it dawned on me that I was going home to an empty house. A feeling of aloneness overpowered me. I felt low in my spirit and broke down in tears.

In that moment I knew that these trips to the gravesite would no longer be enough to hold back the unimaginable loneliness and pain I was feeling. Six feet of dirt may have been set between where I stood and where my husband's body laid, but he was not there. I could have cried out loud telling him how much I missed him but he was not there. I could have fallen on top of the cold ground and laid there all night, but he was not there. I realized I was alone in the cemetery, so I went to the car and locked the doors.

How many of us as Christians truly understand what Jesus went through for us. When He was on the Mount of Olives, and as the sins of the world were being placed upon Him, He began to experience a profound separation between Himself and the Father that eventually broke Him while hanging on the cross. During these moments, even at times when His disciples were with Him, He felt all alone. Although He knew the plan of salvation and what it entailed, He called out to the Father as if there was possible that there may have been some element overlooked. And when the end had come, He grieved an unimaginable grief of separation as He felt total absence from the Father. The spiritual, emotional, and physical consequences of our sins can be witnessed in the gospel accounts.

[In the Garden] *"He withdrew about a stone's throw beyond them, knelt down and prayed, [42] "Father, if you are willing, take this cup from me; yet not my will, but yours be done." [43] An angel from heaven appeared to Him and strengthened Him. [44] And being in anguish, He prayed more earnestly, and his sweat was like drops of blood falling to the ground."*
Luke 22:41-44

[On the Cross] *"And about the ninth hour Jesus cried with a loud voice, saying, Eli, Eli, lama*

sabachthani? That is to say, My God, my God,
why hast thou forsaken me?"
Matthew 27:46

"The Father's presence encircled Christ, and nothing befell Him but that which infinite love permitted for the blessing of the world. Here was His source of comfort, and it is for us. He who is imbued with the Spirit of Christ abides in Christ. The blow that is aimed at him falls upon the Savior, who surrounds him with His presence. Whatever comes to him comes from Christ. He has no need to resist evil, for Christ is his defense. Nothing can touch him except by our Lord's permission, and 'all things' that are permitted 'work together for good to them that love God.' Romans 8:28" Mount of Blessings, Page 71

There I sat at the gravesite in my car. I felt alone but I was not alone. God was with me. He was not just with me but He had prepared me for this very moment. He was the same God of my youth when I was boarding away from home, feeling alone, scared and vulnerable. He was the same God of my young adult years that suffered through the adversity of separation from my husband and family. He was the same God that brought me through the hardships of ministry alongside my husband. He was the same God who brought me through the death of my son. He was the same God who brought me through cancer.

Sitting in the cemetery, in my pain, I was sharing with Christ in the intimacy of affliction, a small taste of the affliction He bore for me; I with Him and He with me. Tonight God was about to talk to me again to allow me realize He is and always will be the God in my afflictions. There I sat, once again in my pain, about to learn what it means to abide in Christ. It would be solidified in my heart that the afflictions that were aimed at me first must fall upon my Savior, who surrounds me with His presence. Whatever affliction that was and will come at me must first go through Christ, therefore it came from Christ. I need not resist this evil, for Christ is my defense. Nothing can touch me except by my Lord's permission. That's why I say 'all things' that are permitted 'work together for good to them that love God.'

As I sat there, I cried out to God, please take these feelings of despair away from me. I opened the bible with no particular scripture in mind, but to my amazement and in answer to my cry, the pages fell open on a random passage. I had not been reading this portion of the bible lately, neither was I familiar with this particular text.

"The righteous perisheth, and no man layeth it to heart and merciful men are taken away, none considering that the righteous is taken away from the evil to come. He shall enter into peace: they shall rest in their beds, each one walking in his uprightness."

Isaiah 57:1,2

I must admit that this was a bit frightening, that God had answered my prayer so promptly. I left that cemetery relieved and at peace. I went home and slept like a baby. I was one greater step closer to finding complete healing and hope as I journey through grief.

Whether you're facing divorce, illness, the death of someone you love, the loss of a job, or financial loss, you will need to let go and trust God with all of your adversities. None of these are easy situations to face nor can we handle them in our own strength. But God promises to give us the courage to face our trials.

"These things I have spoken unto you that in me ye might have peace.
In the world ye might have tribulation:
but be of good cheer, I have overcome the world."
John16:33

Thank God at this point I may not have completed all of the stages of grief, but I can honestly say that my mind is at peace and I live in that great hope of seeing my husband again. God leads the lives of His children. God will do the right thing at the right time and so although we may be in a difficult situation we can still enjoy the present.

One thing that has been a source of strength for me in the challenges of life, is remembering how God has answered my prayers in the past. I have kept a journal for the past 25 years and going over my journal has been a source of strength for me. It's a reminder how God has lead me and helped me through past challenges.

Sometimes when we are faced with trials and we pray, we feel that God does not hear us because He doesn't answer us right away. Let me say that God knows us better than we know ourselves. I believe God delays in answering our prayers at times, because often we are not ready for what He is about to do or we are not in the frame of mind for the answer.

When God answers at the right time it will make a difference in our lives. It will change us for eternity. It will bring not only blessings to us, but to others as well. We will not take what God has done for granted, neither will we take God for granted. Whatever God has blessed us with we should always use it to bless others.

I believe with all my heart that I have experienced these trials and tribulation to build my character for heaven, and also to be a blessing to others and for the glory of God. My prayer therefore is that as I share my story, someone somewhere, even one person, will come to know the loving, merciful and caring God of the universe. He is mindful of every one of His children even me. In God's eyes we are all significant Luke 12:7 describes it saying *"He numbers every hair on our heads"* Luke 12:7.

Thank you God for answering my prayers. They may not be answered according as I desire. However, they are answered according to God's sovereign wisdom in accordance to His will and plan for my life. Life here is not about you or me, it's all about our Lord and Savior Jesus who died to save us.

"But we see Jesus, who was made a little lower than the angels for the suffering of death, crowned with glory and honor; that He by the grace of God should taste death for every man. For it became him, for whom are all things, and by whom are all things, in bringing many sons unto glory, to make the captain of their salvation perfect through sufferings."
Hebrews 2:9-10

If you are suffering today for any reason, whether it's in the death of a loved one, a broken relationship, loss of a job, relationship or suffered financial loss or health, God is able to heal our wounds. God is able to transform us. He can use us to change even the world around us and change our perspective on how we view life and the things that happens to us. Be patient with yourself and with God. When I was a child my mother often use this terminology. "God's mill grinds slow but it grinds to perfection".

Psalm 40:1 says *"I wait patiently for The Lord and He inclined unto me and heard my cry."* God is always on time, He is never too late or too early. He is an on time God. Even in the timely passing of my husband. I asked Him for ten years and he granted my request for which I am eternally grateful. God gave me the time I needed to bond closer with my husband, to grieve during his illness and with the thought of losing him. He has been a merciful and gracious God to me.

In the book *Traveling Light*, New York Times best seller and author, Max Lucado said, "In God's plan every life is long enough and every death is timely enough and though you and I might wish for a longer life, God knows better, ironically, the first to accept God's decision of death is the one who dies." I have seen this played out in my years of nursing with the elderly and very sick patients.

I also realize that my husband had gotten tired and was ready to go. God had prepared me. In that last meaningful conversation we had at the park, when he expressed how he feared leaving me to be alone, we both acknowledged that death was only a sleep and we would see each other again. I gave my husband permission to go. It was not easy, but with God's help I did it. Thank you my love for being a loving, kind, and dedicated Christian husband and father. There is no fear for me being alone, because *"The Lord is my Shepherd I shall not want"* Psalm

23:1. *"A very present help in trouble"* Psalms 46:1. He is the God in my Afflictions.

JESUS MY BEST FRIEND
Bring out the best in me oh Lord!
Bring out the best in me,
the best that is in me to serve You with
sincerity!
You are now The Lord of my life,
I cannot go on without You, You mean
everything to me.
Make me to love others like You do.
Forgive like You forgive,
Even when it hurts to do so!
Bring out the best in me oh Lord
Bring out the best in me.
Even in these painful experiences of life,
may they break me and mould me into Your
likeness.
Oh how much I long to be like You,
oh Lord! I long to be able to trust You as I
ought.
To truly trust You, and be at peace through all
my crucibles.
Yes I will be at peace, because my Jesus cares!
Oh yes He cares
You are my comfort! You are my strength,
You are my provider and protector!
I have had many friends, but none that

understands me like you do!
I love You Jesus; thank you for first loving me!
I feel safe in Your arms! This is where I will stay forever secure.

By Dorreth Mitchell

Chapter 7
The Good in My Afflictions

"And we know that all things work together for good to them that love God, to them who are the called according to His purpose"
Romans 8:28

After the funeral I began to make necessary adjustments to my life. I sold my house with the intention to down size. I rented for a while until something suitable was found. My elderly mother whom we affectionately call mama, was now 93 and was still living with me. I eventually found a small bungalow to accommodate her as I had for so many years before.

Mama was always a source of comfort and support for me. I remember when she first came from Jamaica to Canada to live with us, after my father died. Mama was in her late 60's young, strong, and a widow. I never thought in my wildest dreams that I too would be in my 60's young, strong, and now also a widow.

Over the years Mama would help out in any way she could, cooking, cleaning, and watching the children. Perhaps the greatest source of support was her listening ear, advice and most of all prayers. When tough times would come, I could always depend on her prayers, it was as though she could move heaven and earth on her knees.

My mother was my mentor. She taught me not only how to depend on God on my knees but she also taught me how to be resilient to life changes. Moving from Jamaica to Canada was no easy task. She had to leave her home, her local community, the beautiful sunshine, and her autonomy for a new culture, cold winters, and to now live with her daughter's family as a guest. Yet Mama accepted it all so graciously.

I remember mama walking in her new neighborhood in rain, snow or sunshine. She would walk for miles every day, as she walked she would sing and pray and say hello to our neighbors. This kept her fit and strong. Even into her 80's mama was in such good health, still walking for miles. I remember we use to get large water bottles for our cooler machine. Mama would pick up those 10 gallon water bottles with what seemed like ease, flipping it over into the cooler.

Now in her 90's her age and health began to deteriorate. While Mitch was still alive she had a stroke, she did recover, but never returning to full health. Mama was strong enough however to be a help to Mitch especially when his strength was going down. I don't know how I could have done it without her. Having to go to work I knew she would be able to bring him food, and even call 911 when he had some close calls.

It was her pleasure to be there for Mitch as he had always welcomed her into his home with open arms. I have always been so appreciative of Mitch's support of having my mother living with us. Mama's relationship with him was as though she was his own mother and Mitch her very own son.

After Mitch died Mama lived with me for one year, but with failing health and strength I had to find a nursing home for her so she could have full-time care.

Most days after leaving work or before I went to work, I would stop and visit my mother in the nursing home. I looked forward to the day when I could be able to spend more quality time with her. Putting my mother in the nursing was a big decision for me, but her resilience in accepting life changes put me at peace. Thank God for her.

Six weeks after my husband died I returned to work. That was so difficult for me. In all my working life while Mitch was healthy he had always driven me to work, and picked me up. It's not that I couldn't drive, he just enjoyed driving me so much. During the latter part of his illness I had begun to drive myself to work, it was still comforting just to know that Mitch was at home even though he no longer was driving. We would talk on the phone, so that I would not fall asleep. Working my shifts at work then coming home and taking care of Mitch was wearing on my body, but love drove me to push my body to its limits.

But after his death it became unbearable driving back and forth from my job in downtown Toronto to Brampton. In addition, work life had become more challenging than ever. I was now beginning to find working full-time a chore. My profession as a registered nurse, that I found so fulfilling and rewarding at one time, now became burdensome. I made up my mind right there and then that I would retire within five years. Because I had suffered a major financial loss I had to work for another five years.

I prayed to God to give me the wisdom patience and tolerance I needed to cope. I made up my mind to enjoy the rest of my working years, to give of my best to my patients, and to minister to them as Jesus would. As challenging as it was, I did it with God's help. God in His faithfulness rewarded my obedience.

Thank God I retired in October 2014. A few months after my retirement, my mother suffered another stroke. Having been retired, I was now able to spend that quality time with her that I had prayed for. Talk about God's perfect timing. My mother did not survive, she experienced a lot of complications and eventually passed away on February 28, 2015 at 98 years of age.

We thank God as a family for the many precious years we had with her. I particularly thank God that I was already retired so that I could give her that personal care she needed in this frail stage of her life. My praise will continually go up to God who has been my source of comfort.

Taking care of Mitch before his death, and taking care of Mama directly after, really took a toll on my health. In 2014, six months before my actual date of retirement, I took two weeks off work to attend my nephew's wedding in Santa Monica, California. Upon my return home, my bowels felt sluggish so I decided to take a herbal cleansing the day before I returned to work.

This herbal cleansing did not work as expected and that particular morning I ended up in the hospital emergency. I was required to do a colonoscopy which resulted in me discovering that I had stage 2 colon cancer.

Upon hearing the diagnosis I thought why now? Six month before retirement? I was prepared to die, but I did not sense that my life on this earth was over. I did think however what implications will this have on my retirement. If I retired early it would significantly impact my financial plans for retirement. By now I had learned to trust God in everything.

"Be anxious for nothing, but in everything by prayer and supplication, with thanksgiving, let

your requests be made known to God; [7] *and the peace of God, which surpasses all understanding, will guard your hearts and minds through Christ Jesus"*
Philippians 4:6, 7

To make a long story short, I have since had it surgically removed with no further treatment required, except for follow up appointments and a yearly colonoscopy. This is indeed my second chance for life. There are always forks in the road of life. I thank God, because it could have been worse.

If I hadn't taken that herbal cleansing my symptoms could have gone on unnoticed, and it could have been too late. I thank God that today, this minute, I am alive and I have a second chance for a longer life as I pay special attention to my health. Thanks to the mercy and grace of God. I am conscious of the fact that my purpose on this earth is to be a blessing and to live to glorify God.

After my husband's death I felt helpless and hopeless. After my diagnosis of cancer I decided to give God total control of leading my life through this painful passage of grief, meaning even in my appetite. I would permit no other earthly pleasure, not even food, to replace the role of comforter that belonged to God. And God has not let me down.

You see in every trouble that confronts us, God wants to help us through, it and for us to come up higher in Him, stronger in our faith. This life is not about us. It's about our character and our will being stronger in Christ.

In my cancer diagnosis God was saying to me, slow down my child. I want you to pay special attention to the laws of health and to how you treat your body. God has given us direct instructions in His word of all that He expects of us.

"Know ye not that ye are the temple of God and that the Spirit of God dwells in you?
If any man defile the temple of God, him shall God destroy,
for the temple of God is holy which temple ye are."
1 Corinthians 3:16-17

God's desire for us is that if we live, we live for Him and if we die, we die in Him. Whatever we do should bring honor and glory to God as suggested in 1 Corinthians 10:31. I have since been paying special attention to the laws of health. The bottom line is not whether I live or die, that's not the reason why we are here. We are here to be a blessing to humanity and in so doing bring honor and glory to God. We must be mindful that we will not live forever and our loved ones will not live forever.

"For all flesh is as grass and all the glory of man as the flower of grass. The grass withereth and the flower therefore fadeth away. But the word of the Lord endure forever and this is the word which by the gospel is preached unto you."

I Peter 1: 24-25

It is a new year, 2016 approaching 6 years since the passing of my husband. I have become accustomed to adversity through losses. Most recently my son and daughter-in-law who were a great support to me have recently relocated to the USA and no longer live in close proximity. God however, in His love and mercy allowed all these events to take place in a timely manner so that I could digest it and be able to accept it favorably. I have accepted all of these changes as all part of God's plan for our lives. I thank God for them and accept them with composure.

We all know the story of Job and how he experienced great troubles, when losing everything he possessed including his health. No doubt this was difficult for him, but Job accepted it with equanimity until his friends came to discourage him. In this life we have to be very careful of the friends we keep or of those we share our troubles with. Have they been with Jesus? Will they encourage you into seeking a deeper connection with The Lord?

Unlike Job, I have had wonderful support through family, friends, along with brothers and sisters in the ministry. Through these friendships and support systems I have learned to discover my life purpose.

I believed that the main purpose for me to have experienced these difficult times in my life as a child of God did not just happen by chance. You see because life is not really about us, anything that happens to a child of God has been divinely worked out ahead by God. Now is the time for me to celebrate my troubles through trusting that the God who has comforted me in my afflictions is in fact guiding my life. I have a passion to share my testimony to bless others.

The first opportunity was given to me by Sister Grace McDonald, the health ministry leader at my home church, Brampton Seventh-day Adventist church. I realized then how important it was for me to accept sharing my testimony as a vital part of this transition in my life.

This lead to God opening up another opportunity through sister Sharon Edwards, the first lady of the Ontario Conference. Her ministry has been instrumental in facilitating opportunities for pastors' families, especially the wives, to bond and feel the sisterhood support. In compassion, she continued to reach out to me even after my husband's passing. When she asked me to share my testimony with my sisters in ministry one year, I was delighted to do so.

A few months later my dear sister in Christ, Purtine Morris, who has been a great support to me, asked me to address the ladies in her women's ministry group at her church. Purtine has also asked me to speak at her women's ministry day at the

Downsview Seventh-day Adventist church, on another occasion. God has opened up this opportunity for me to bring comfort and healing to those who are wounded with the trials of this life. Sharing my woes has also helped me to process my own fears. It is also for this reason that I write my story so that I can share with others the love of God the Father for us His children.

If I had not been afflicted I would not have called on the Lord, and He would not have answered me. I love when Jesus Christ answers me, and affirms my faith in Him. Because my God has answered me I cannot help but declare, "it is good for me that I was afflicted." I have learned to depend on Him for everything. That kind of faith pleases Him, that's why I cannot help but declare, "it is good for me that I was afflicted." I have learned to trust Him more even when I cannot see the way. It has given me peace of mind even in the storm, that's why I cannot help but declare, "it is good for me that I was afflicted."

I have learned to praise Him in all my circumstances, no matter how hard they may be, and my heart is so content. That's why I cannot help but declare, "it is good for me that I was afflicted."

I have learned to fall on my face and demonstrate true sorrow for my sins. Through this I have learned the forgiving and merciful character of God. He draws me closer in my humility, that's why I cannot help but declare "it is good for me that I was afflicted."

"It is good for me that I was afflicted," because now I have a greater appreciation for family and friends.

"It is good for me that I was afflicted," because now I am strengthened to honor my body as the temple of God.

"It is good for me that I was afflicted," because now I do not have any delusions of my mortality. I do not take my life for granted.

"It is good for me that I was afflicted," as I have lost many loved ones, and have faced death myself. I now have no fear of it, because I know Whose hands I am in.

"It is good for me that I was afflicted," because now I am not afraid to live in my purpose, and to share my faith.

"It is good for me that I was afflicted," because now I am not afraid to be in the garden alone with God, content with His company.

Yes I have been afflicted, but when I look at all that God has done for me, all that He is doing in me, and how He is working through me, I cannot help but declare like David, "it is good for me that I was afflicted."

All these things and more are the good in my afflictions.

Conclusion

"He delivers the afflicted by their affliction and opens their ear by adversity."
Job 36:15

Although Job lost everything, God restored to him two times what had been taken away. It is noted that with his children he received the same amount of sons and daughters he previously had, but not doubled as his livestock and other material blessings. It is commonly believed that God had done so as an assurance to Job and his wife that they would one day be united back with their entire family at the resurrection, both previous children and along with the new children. In this understanding his children were also double, revealing that God never takes away without restoring, when we walk in obedience to His will.

Today I look forward to reuniting with all the loved ones in my life that have passed away, especially my son and husband. I look forward to that grand union where those of us who are still alive will be caught up to meet them in the air.

"For the Lord Himself shall descend from heaven with a shout, with the voice of the archangel, and with the trump of God: and the dead in Christ shall rise first:

17 Then we which are alive and remain shall be caught up together with them in the clouds, to meet the Lord in the air: and so shall we ever be with the Lord."

1 Thessalonians 4:16, 17

Who are we to question how we receive our deliverance? Since we all are delivered through Christ afflictions, if He sees fit to prepare us for eternity with a measure of adversity, then we must accept that yoke with an open heart. When time is no more, we will receive all that is lost and much more. I invite you to take the first step today and declare "It is good for me that I was afflicted"

Made in the USA
Charleston, SC
23 September 2016